DK EYEWITNESS WORKBOOKS
Rocks & Minerals

by Helen Whittaker

DK | Penguin Random House

Educational Consultants Linda B. Gambrell
and Geraldine Taylor

Senior Editors Susan Reuben, Fleur Star
Assistant Editor Lisa Stock
Editor Anuroop Sanwalia
US Senior Editor Shannon Beatty
Art Editors Peter Laws, Simon Murrell, Tanisha Mandal
DK Picture Library Claire Bowers, Lucy Claxton,
Rose Horridge, Myriam Megharbi, Romaine Werblow
Managing Editors Christine Stroyan, Shikha Kulkarni
Managing Art Editors Anna Hall, Govind Mittal
DTP Designer Anita Yadav
Production Editor Tom Morse
Production Controller Rachel Ng
Senior Jacket Designer Suhita Dharamjit
Jacket Design Development Manager Sophia MTT
Publisher Andrew Macintyre
Art Director Karen Self
Publishing Director Jonathan Metcalf

This American Edition, 2020
First American Edition, 2008
Published in the United States by DK Publishing
1450 Broadway, Suite 801, New York, NY 10018

DK books are available at special discounts when purchased in bulk
for sales, promotions, premiums, fund-raising, or educational use.
For details, contact: DK Publishing Special Markets,
1450 Broadway, Suite 801, New York, NY 10018.
SpecialSales@dk.com

Printed and bound in Canada

For the curious

www.dk.com

Contents

Fast Facts

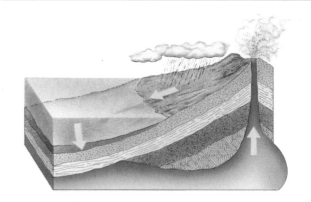

Activities

Quick Quiz

How This Book Can Help Your Child

Eyewitness Workbooks offer a fun and colorful range of stimulating titles in the subjects of history, science, and geography. Devised and written with the expert advice of educational consultants, each workbook aims to:

• develop a child's knowledge of a popular topic
• provide practice of key skills and reinforce classroom learning
• nurture a child's special interest in a subject.

About this book

Eyewitness Workbook Rocks & Minerals is an activity-packed exploration of the rocks and minerals that shape our world. Inside you will find:

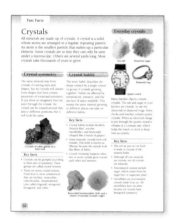  

Fast Facts

This section presents key information as concise facts, which are easy to digest, learn, and remember. Encourage your child to start by reading through the valuable information in the Fast facts section and studying the statistics charts at the back of the book before trying out the activities.

Activities

The enjoyable, fill-in activities are designed to develop information recall and help your child practice cross-referencing skills. Each activity can be completed using information provided on the page, in the Fast facts section, or on the charts at the back of the book.

Quick Quiz

There are six pages of multiple-choice questions to test your child's new-found knowledge of the subject. Children should only try answering the quiz questions once all of the activity section has been completed.

Important information

• Please ensure that your child wears gloves and goggles when handling the epsom salts in the stalactite growing activity on page 21.

• You will also need to help your child use the scratching tools suggested in the hardness test activity on page 31.

• Rock hunting is fun, but you should accompany your child to make sure they follow the safety advice on page 33.

PROGRESS CHART

Chart your progress as you work through the activity and quiz pages in this book.
First check your answers, then color in a star in the correct box below.

Page	Topic	Star	Page	Topic	Star	Page	Topic	Star
14	Volcano!	☆	24	Building Stones	☆	34	Identifying Specimens	☆
15	Weathering and Erosion	☆	25	Coal	☆	35	Identifying Specimens	☆
16	Transportation and Deposition	☆	26	Gemstones	☆	36	Geological Timeline	☆
17	Rocks on the Beach	☆	27	Metals	☆	37	Geological Timeline	☆
18	Metamorphism	☆	28	Precious Metals	☆	38	Rocks	☆
19	Rock Story	☆	29	Other Uses for Rocks and Minerals	☆	39	All Sorts of Fossils	☆
20	Famous Rock Formations	☆	30	Properties of Minerals	☆	40	Using Rocks and Minerals	☆
21	Limestone Landscapes	☆	31	Properties of Minerals	☆	41	Describing Minerals	☆
22	Mining and Quarrying	☆	32	Cutting and Polishing	☆	42	Metals and Ores	☆
23	Rocks as Tools	☆	33	Collecting Rocks	☆	43	Gemstones	☆

Planet Earth

Earth is a rocky planet. The study of the rocks and minerals Earth is made of is called geology, and scientists who specialize in geology are called geologists. By studying rocks and minerals, geologists can figure out what the planet might have been like long ago and improve their understanding of the forces that continue to shape it today.

Rock or mineral?

A mineral is a naturally occuring, solid substance. A rock is a combination of one or more minerals. Some rocks are made up almost entirely of one mineral. Other rocks are made up of many different minerals. Rocks and minerals provide us with many useful resources.

Diamond

Gold

Rocks containing diamond and gold

Key facts

- Rocks and minerals have many uses—as building materials, as fuel, in medicines, jewelry, makeup, and even in food!
- The most expensive minerals by weight are diamond and painite.
- Diamond is also the hardest mineral on Earth.

In the beginning

The early solar system

Earth and the other planets formed from the solar nebula, a huge disk of gas and dust left over from the formation of the Sun. Nearer the Sun, where gravity was stronger, heavier elements gathered together to form the rocky inner planets. Further out, where gravity was weaker, lighter elements formed the gas giants.

Key facts

- The planets in our solar system began forming about 4.6 billion years ago.
- Earth is the largest of the four rocky inner planets. The other rocky planets are Mercury, Venus, and Mars.
- The Sun accounts for about 99.86 percent of the entire mass of the solar system.

Inside story

Earth's outer layer, the crust, varies in depth from 5 to 43 miles (7 to 70 km). Below this, the mantle reaches to a depth of about 1,793 miles (2,885 km). Next comes the liquid outer core, made of iron and nickel. At the center of the planet is the inner core, a solid ball of iron 1,516 miles (2,440 km) in diameter.

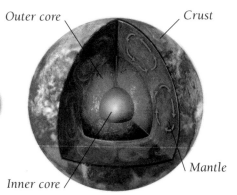

Outer core   *Crust*

Inner core   *Mantle*

Cross-section of Earth

Key facts

- Scientists know about the different layers inside Earth from studying how seismic waves (vibrations produced by earthquakes) travel through the ground.
- The mantle is the largest layer. It makes up about 84 percent of Earth's volume.
- In the mantle, temperatures range between 930°F–1,652°F (500°C–900°C) near the crust to over 7,200°F (4,000°C) near the outer core.
- The soft rocks of the mantle are moving all the time. They flow slowly from cooler areas near the crust to hotter areas near the core and back again.

The Rock Cycle

Earth's rocks are continually forming, wearing down, and re-forming. This process is known as the rock cycle. Some parts of the rock cycle, such as volcanoes erupting and cliffs wearing away, happen fairly quickly and can be seen directly. However, many of the processes involved in the rock cycle are hidden away underground and take millions of years to complete.

Rock changes

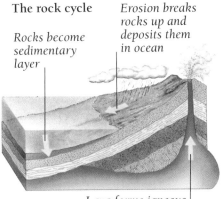

The rock cycle

Rocks become sedimentary layer

Erosion breaks rocks up and deposits them in ocean

Lava forms igneous rock on surface

Rocks on the move

This model shows Earth's major tectonic plates. The red dots represent areas of volcanic activity.

Earth's upper layers (the crust and the top part of the mantle) are made up of separate pieces, called tectonic plates. These are constantly moving, fueled by the planet's inner heat. Tectonic plate movements push rocks down, push them up to form mountain ranges, and create areas of volcanic activity.

Key facts

- Tectonic plates move between 0.4 and 6 in (1 and 15 cm) per year.
- Places where two or more plates meet are called plate boundaries.
- There are three types of plate boundary: convergent, where plates push together, divergent, where they pull apart, and transform, where they push past each other.

Volcanic activity

When a volcano erupts, molten (liquid) rock, called magma, moves from deep underground to the surface. When magma erupts onto the surface as a liquid, it is called lava. But it may also be blasted into the air, turning into tiny pieces of solid rock called ash, or much larger globs called volcanic "bombs."

Key facts

- Most of the world's active volcanoes are found on tectonic plate boundaries.
- There are three main types of volcano: stratovolcanoes, cinder cones, and shield volcanoes. Stratovolcanoes and cinder cones erupt explosively, and shield volcanoes have nonexplosive eruptions.

Minor eruptions on Gunung Batur, a stratovolcano in Bali, Indonesia

As soon as rocks are exposed at Earth's surface they begin to be eroded (worn away). Particles of eroded rock are transported (carried away) by water, wind, or ice. They eventually settle as sediment, which in time forms sedimentary rocks (see page 8). As new layers of sediment are laid down, the original rock gets deeper. The weight of rocks above causes an increase in pressure and temperature, which gradually changes the rock. Rocks formed in this way are called metamorphic rocks (see page 8).

Key facts

- There are many forces that cause erosion, including wind, rain, flowing water, waves, glaciers, and changes in temperature.
- The process by which sediment is laid down is known as deposition.
- The process by which rocks are changed by heat and pressure is called metamorphism.

Types of Rock

One way of classifying rocks is according to how they were formed. Rocks created by volcanic activity are known as igneous (from the Latin meaning "fiery"). Rocks made from compressed layers of sediment are sedimentary, and rocks formed when changes in temperature or pressure cause one type of rock to change into another are called metamorphic.

Igneous rocks

Igneous rocks may be formed underground or above ground. Igneous rocks formed underground often have large crystals. (See the picture of granite on page 9.) Lava from an erupting volcano forms igneous rocks above ground. These rocks may be smooth and shiny like obsidian, or dull and full of holes like pumice.

Black obsidian   *Pumice*

Obsidian is formed from rapidly cooling lava rich in silicate minerals (see page 9). Pumice is formed from frothy lava.

Key facts

• Igneous rocks formed underground are known as intrusive. Those formed above ground are called extrusive.

• Extrusive rocks can be formed from volcanic ash as well as lava.

• Some examples of igneous rocks are granite, gabbro, and basalt.

Sedimentary rocks

Because sedimentary rocks are built up gradually, as layer upon layer of sediment is laid down, these layers can often be seen in the rock. Sedimentary rocks may be made up of broken rock fragments, seashells, or evaporites (minerals left behind when mineral-rich water evaporates).

Key facts

• Sediments are converted into rock by the process of lithification. Heat and pressure caused by the weight of new layers of sediment above make the particles of sediment stick together and become harder.

• Layers of sedimentary rock are called strata.

• Some examples of sedimentary rocks are sandstone and shale.

Sandstone   **Sandstone formed from sand, and shale formed from mud and clay**

Shale

Metamorphic rocks

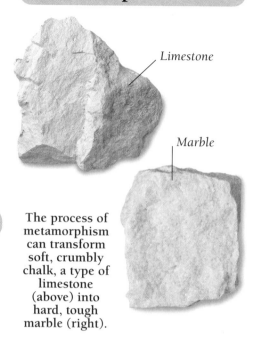

Limestone

Marble

The process of metamorphism can transform soft, crumbly chalk, a type of limestone (above) into hard, tough marble (right).

Existing rocks altered by extreme heat and pressure, or by extreme heat alone, are called metamophic rocks. As the existing rocks are crushed and heated, new minerals gradually grow from the elements present in the rock, and these eventually combine to form an entirely new type of rock.

Key facts

• Some examples of metamorphic rocks are marble, slate, schist, and gneiss.

• Metamorphic rocks can be classified according to their texture. Granular rocks have an even, grainy texture. Foliated rocks have distinct bands in different colors.

• Metamorphic changes may take place where rocks are deeply buried, where rocks are heated by nearby magma, where rocks are pushed together at tectonic plate boundaries, and where rocks are heated by a meteorite impact.

Rock-forming Minerals

Elements are the basic building blocks of all matter. Just eight elements (oxygen, silicon, aluminum, iron, calcium, sodium, potassium, and magnesium) make up about 99 percent of Earth's crust. These and other elements combine to form the minerals that, in turn, combine to create rocks. Rock-forming minerals are classified according to the elements they are made from.

Minerals in rocks

In some types of rock, the mineral crystals are fairly big and you may be able to see the different minerals that make up the rock. If you look at a piece of granite, for example, you can see the individual crystals of quartz, mica, and feldspar that it is made from.

Quartz

Granite

Feldspar

Mica

Granite, with the minerals it is made from: quartz, mica, and feldspar

Silicate minerals

Silicate minerals are rich in the elements silicon and oxygen. Silicate minerals are the largest and most important class of rock-forming minerals because there are so many of them and because most of Earth's mantle and crust is made of them. Common silicates include feldspar, quartz, olivine, pyroxene, amphibole, and mica.

Key facts

Olivine, a silicate of iron and magnesium

- Geologists have discovered more than 600 different types of silicate minerals.
- Silicate minerals are found in a wide range of rock types.
- The rocks of the Moon and the other rocky planets are also made mainly of silicate minerals.
- The gemstones topaz, emerald, and aquamarine are single crystals of silicate minerals (see page 10).

Carbonate minerals

Carbonate minerals are rich in the elements carbon and oxygen. The commonest carbonate mineral is calcite. Calcite is the main mineral that makes up the rock limestone. Limestone cave systems and their stalactite and stalagmite formations are made almost entirely of calcite. Calcite is also the main mineral in the rock marble.

Key facts

- The calcite in the rock limestone comes from the shells of dead sea creatures.
- There are more than 800 different forms of calcite crystal.
- Limestone caves form because the mineral calcite dissolves in rainwater.

Dolomite, a carbonate mineral

Key facts

- Pure quartz is colorless, but various impurities give it a range of colors. Although quartz is very common, some colors of the mineral are valued as semi-precious gems.
- Some types of mica split easily into thin, clear sheets. They were once used as window panes.
- Feldspars are very common minerals, making up about 40 percent of Earth's crust.

Crystals

All minerals are made up of crystals. A crystal is a solid whose atoms are arranged in a regular, repeating pattern. An atom is the smallest particle that makes up a particular element. Some crystals are so tiny they can only be seen under a microscope. Others are several yards long. Most crystals take thousands of years to grow.

Everyday crystals

Sea salt   Demerera sugar

Diamond ring

Quartz watch

Crystal symmetry

The same mineral may form crystals of varying sizes and shapes, but its crystals will always form shapes that have certain properties of rotational symmetry. If you drew an imaginary line (an axis) through the crystal, the crystal can be rotated around that axis to different positions, but it will look the same.

Crystals of cubic galena on a host rock

Key facts

- Crystals can be grouped according to their axes of symmetry. These groups are called crystal systems.
- There are seven crystal systems. From least to most symmetrical, they are triclinic, monoclinic, orthorhombic, rhombohedral (also called trigonal), tetragonal, hexagonal, and cubic.

Crystal habits

The term 'habit' describes the shape created by a single crystal or group of crystals growing together. Habits are affected by temperature, pressure, and the amount of space available. This means the same mineral growing in different places can take on different habits.

Key facts

- Crystal habits include dendritic (branch-like), acicular (needlelike), and botryoidal (shaped like a bunch of grapes).
- Some minerals' crystals form soft strands. This habit is known as 'fibrous' because the crystals look like fibers of fabric.
- Crystal 'twinning' happens when two or more crystals grow toward each other and intersect.

Botryoidal hemimorphite (left) and a cluster of acicular crystals (right)

Many familiar objects contain crystals. The salt and sugar in your kitchen are crystals. So are the diamonds in diamond rings. Many clocks and watches contain quartz crystals. When an electrical charge is put through the quartz crystal it vibrates at a constant rate, which helps the watch or clock to keep time accurately.

Key facts

- The salt we put on our food is made of crystals of the mineral halite.
- Although all true minerals are crystals, not all crystals are minerals.
- Non-mineral crystals include sugar, which comes from the sugar beet or sugarcane plant.
- Snowflakes are non-mineral crystals made from ice. All snowflakes have six arms because ice crystals have hexagonal symmetry.

Ores

An ore is a rock containing valuable mineral deposits that are economically profitable to extract. Some of the most important and widely mined ores are metal ores. Like most other minerals, metals can be found in more than one rock type, so they can come from more than one kind of ore.

Hematite

Hematite is the main ore of iron, which is the most widely used metal. Iron accounts for about 95 percent of metal tonnage produced worldwide. An alloy is a mixture that includes one or more metals. Steel, an iron alloy, is used extensively in construction and manufacturing.

Key facts

Hematite

Stainless steel measuring cups

- Hematite gets its name from the Greek word *haima*, meaning "blood," because it is often red in color.
- The second most important iron ore is magnetite. It is the most magnetic naturally occurring mineral on Earth.
- Humans have been mining iron ore for at least three and a half thousand years.

Chalcopyrite

Chalcopyrite is the commonest ore of copper. Copper is soft, easily formed, and is a good conductor of electricity. It is used in electrical wiring, in plumbing pipes and fittings, in cookware, and in coins. The most important alloys of copper are bronze (copper and tin) and brass (copper and zinc).

Key facts

- .Copper is one of very few metals that can be widely found in its native state. This means it is found on its own, rather than combined with other minerals in an ore:
- For this reason, copper was one of the first metals to be used by humans.
- Because copper conducts heat evenly it is often used on the bottom of saucepans.

Chalcopyrite

Electrical cable, showing the copper wires inside

Bauxite

Bauxite ore is the main source of aluminum. Aluminum conducts electricity well, is lightweight, and resists corrosion. It has many uses, including making power lines, aircraft, drinks cans, and cooking utensils. In fact, aluminum is the second most widely used metal after iron.

Key facts

Bauxite

Aluminum kitchen foil

- Aluminum is the most abundant metal on Earth.
- Aluminum is almost never found in its native state. Instead, it occurs as compounds (combined with other chemical elements) in various ores.
- Aluminum compounds are used in the production of glass and ceramics, and in the manufacture of jet fuel, paints, and antiperspirants.
- Other important metal ores include sphalerite (zinc), nickeline (nickel), cassiterite (tin), galena (lead), and cinnabar (mercury).
- Bauxite was named after Les Beaux-de-Provence in France, where it was first discovered in 1821.

11

Fossils

Fossils are evidence of past life preserved in rocks. True fossils are the remains of animals and plants. Trace fossils consist of other evidence, such as droppings or footprints. Because the process of fossilization begins when remains or traces become buried by sediment, most fossils are found in sedimentary rocks. Limestones and shales are especially rich sources.

Fossil formation

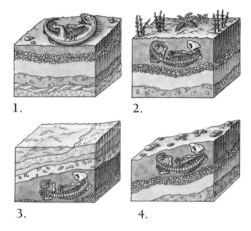

1. 2.

3. 4.

1. An animal dies.
2. Its remains are covered by sediment.
3. In time, rock-forming minerals replace the original minerals in the bone. The skeleton is now a fossil.
4. Tectonic plate movements and erosion eventually bring the fossil to the surface.

Key facts

- The word fossil comes from the Latin *fossus*, meaning "having been dug up."
- Early fossil hunters often used explosives to find specimens.
- Most animal and plant remains do not become fossilized. Instead they simply decay.

All sorts of fossils

Because sedimentary rocks are laid down all over Earth's surface, the fossils they contain represent plants and animals from a wide variety of habitats. Amber (hardened tree resin) is another source of fossils. Many samples of amber contain living things trapped in the sticky resin as it flowed, such as leaves, flowers, insects, and spiders.

Fossilized sea star in sandstone

Compound leaf, fossilized in mudstone

Spider in amber

Key facts

- Fossils have been found that range from several thousand to several billion years old.
- The earliest known fossils are of bacteria.
- The science of paleontology (the study of fossils) began in the late 18th century.

Dinosaurs

Dinosaurs were a large and varied group of land-dwelling animals that dominated the planet for more than 130 million years. Almost everything scientists know about dinosaurs has been discovered by studying fossils. The first dinosaurs appeared about 235 million years ago, during the Triassic period. They became extinct at the end of the Cretaceous period, about 65 million years ago.

Complete dinosaur skeletons like this *Gryposaurus* embedded in clay are rare.

Key facts

- The word dinosaur was coined by the English paleontologist Richard Owen in 1842. It comes from two Greek words meaning "fearsome reptile."
- Dinosaur remains have been found on every continent on Earth, including Antarctica.
- Dinosaurs are divided into two orders: Saurischian (meaning lizard-hipped) and Ornithischian (meaning bird-hipped).
- Modern birds evolved from a group of dinosaurs called the theropods, part of the lizard-hipped Saurischian order.
- The dinosaurs were wiped out by a sudden disaster, most probably a massive asteroid impact.

Rocks from Space

There are four rocky planets in the solar system and hundreds of thousands of smaller rocky bodies. Scientists have learned a lot about the minerals they contain from pieces of space rock that have fallen to Earth as meteorites, from observations through telescopes, from photos taken by spacecraft, and from surface exploration of the Moon and Mars.

Meteorites

Meteoroids, pieces of rocky debris left over from the formation of the solar system, frequently come close enough to Earth to be pulled in by its gravity. When a meteoroid enters the atmosphere it burns brightly and is known as a meteor. A meteorite is a portion of a meteoroid that survives the descent through the atmosphere.

Key facts

- Most meteoroids break up completely when entering Earth's atmosphere.
- Nevertheless, each year an estimated 500 meteorites hit the ground.
- Only a very small number of meteorites are large enough to create an impact crater.

Fragments from the Canyon Diablo meteorite

Moon rocks

Sample of Moon rock

The Apollo 12 Lunar Module landing on the Moon

Unlike Earth, the Moon does not have an active rock cycle, because it lacks tectonic plates and an atmosphere. This means the rocks on its surface are much older than those on Earth's surface.

Key facts

- Astronauts walked on the Moon during six Apollo missions from 1969 to 1972 (Apollo 11 to Apollo 17). They collected 2,415 samples of Moon rock, weighing a total of 842 lb (382 kg).
- The Apollo 11 crew discovered a new mineral on the Moon. Scientists named it armalcolite, in honor of the astronauts **Arm**strong, **Ald**rin, and **Col**lins.

Rocks on Mars

We know a lot about the rocks on Mars from photographs taken by spacecraft in orbit around the planet, and from photographs and rock samples taken by robotic rovers on its surface. The surface of Mars is mainly made of basalt. Large areas are covered by a fine dust of iron oxide, which is what gives the planet its reddish color.

Key facts

- Evidence in the rocks on Mars shows that billions of years ago the planet was volcanically active and water flowed on its surface. Now it is geologically dead and completely dry. Most of the planet's remaining water is trapped in the polar ice caps.
- NASA's Mars Exploration Rovers, *Spirit* and *Opportunity*, explored Mars from 2004 until 2010 (*Spirit*) and 2018 (*Opportunity*).
- NASA, ESA (the European Space Agency), and Russia are all planning to send humans to Mars.
- Scientists believe that some meteorites found on Earth originated from Mars.

Artist's impression of one of the Mars Exploration Rovers

Volcano!

A volcanic vent is an opening through which lava and other volcanic materials erupt. The vent is linked via a tunnel called a conduit to a chamber containing magma (molten rock). A volcano is a mountain created from layers of material laid down over many eruptions.

Lava pours into the ocean from a volcano in Hawaii.

Inside a volcano

Use the information on this page to help you label this diagram with the words in the list below. Choose from:

magma chamber   conduit   ash cloud   lava flow
eruption at central vent   eruption at side vent
strata (layers from previous eruption)

4. ....

1. ....
....

5. ....
....

2. ....

6. ....
....

3. ....

7. ....

Identify the volcano

Look at the pictures below, then read the descriptions. Can you match the caption to the correct picture?

1.
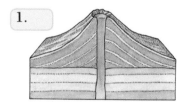

2.
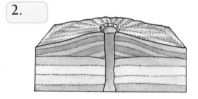

3.
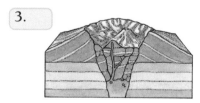

a. A **cinder cone** is made by magma that explodes into the air, creating tiny rock fragments called cinders. Many cinder cones have a bowl-shaped crater.

b. A **stratovolcano** has steeply sloping sides. It is created by viscous (thick) magma that moves slowly and cools quickly. Its eruptions are explosive.

c. A **shield volcano** has gently sloping sides. It is created by runny magma that moves quickly and cools slowly. Its eruptions are effusive (nonexplosive).

Weathering and Erosion

Weathering and erosion play an important part in the rock cycle because they are the two main processes that break down rocks. Weathering happens when rocks break down where they stand. Erosion occurs when material is carried away by water, wind, or ice. The two processes often take place at the same time.

Facts

- Moving water, ice, and air all wear away rock. This is known as abrasion.
- Flowing water in streams and rivers carves out valleys, and over time can create deep, steep-sided valleys called gorges (also known as canyons).
- The motion of the ocean's waves erodes coastal rocks.
- Glaciers can carry huge rocks, called erratic boulders, vast distances.
- In deserts the main cause of erosion is particles of sand carried by the wind.
- Various gases in the air react with rainwater to form a weak acid, which corrodes (dissolves) rock. Corrosion is particularly bad in cities because of air pollution.
- Freeze-thaw is a cycle of freezing and thawing in places with large temperature variations. When water trapped in rocks freezes it expands, breaking the rock apart. Scree (loose rock on mountains) is created by freeze-thaw.

What caused it?

Draw a line to match each rock with the most likely cause of weathering or erosion. Use the information on the right to help you.

1. An erratic boulder

2. Coastal rocks

3. Stone carving

wave action

a glacier

corrosion

freeze-thaw

wind-borne particles

flowing water

4. Desert rock

5. Scree slope

6. Grand Canyon

Weathering and erosion puzzle

Circle the right word to complete these sentences about weathering and erosion, using the information on this page and on page 7 to help you.

1. Weathering and erosion play an important part in the rock cycle because they **build rocks up / break rocks down / make new rocks.**
2. Rock is abraded when it is **worn away / dissolved / frozen.**
3. Rock is corroded when it is **worn away / dissolved / frozen.**
4. The process of freeze-thaw happens in environments where there is **no / a small / a large** variation in temperature.
5. In deserts most erosion is caused by **water / wind / ice.**

Transportation and Deposition

Eroded rocks are transported by wind, water, or ice and deposited somewhere else. Rivers play an important role in this by carrying sediment in the form of gravel, sand, silt, soil, and clay. As rivers get wider, they slow down. More and more sediment falls out of the water and is deposited (dropped) on the riverbed.

The mud in this river mouth was deposited by the river water.

Fast water, slow water

Try this experiment to find out how the speed at which water is flowing affects how much sediment is deposited.

You need:
- *3 jam jars*
- *measuring cup*
- *water*
- *soil*
- *3 teaspoons*
- *a friend*

1 Pour the same volume of water into three different glass jars.

2 Put the same amount of soil in each jar and label the jars 1 to 3.

3 With the help of a friend, stir the water in all three jars quickly with a teaspoon until all the soil is moving.

4 Stop stirring the water in jar 1 and continue to stir the water in jar 2, but slowly. Ask your friend to keep on stirring the water in jar 3 quickly.

5 Continue in the same way for a couple of minutes, observing what happens to the soil in all three jars.

In which jar did the most soil fall to the bottom? ....
Complete the sentences, using the words "more" or "less."
The faster the water is moving, the .... sediment is deposited.
The slower the water is moving, the .... sediment is deposited.

River facts

- The sediment carried by a river is called its load, and includes stones and boulders, which it rolls along the river bed, and sand, clay, and silt carried in suspension (hanging in the water).

- The faster a river flows, the more sediment it can carry. When river water slows down, sediment drops out of suspension.

- River water moves faster near the source and more slowly near the mouth because the terrain becomes less steep, and the channel through which the river flows becomes broader.

True or false?

Using the information on this page, check the boxes to show which of these facts are true and which are false.

	TRUE	FALSE
1. Rivers play an important part in transportation and deposition.	☐	☐
2. Most of the sediment carried by a river is deposited near its source.	☐	☐
3. The sediment carried by a river is called its load.	☐	☐
4. The faster water flows, the less sediment it can carry.	☐	☐
5. As well as water, wind and ice can transport and deposit rock.	☐	☐

Rocks on the Beach

At the beach you can see the rock cycle in action. Many seashores are backed by cliffs. At their base, rocks that have fallen from above, loosened by weathering, are eroded by the ocean, and deposited into areas of pebbles, gravel, sand, and mud.

Seashore rock formations

Use the information on this page to help you label this photo with the words in the list below.
Choose from:

cliffs   sand
boulder   headland
stumps   bay
shingle

1. ....

2. ....

3. ....

4. ....

5. ....

6. ....

7. ....

Seashore rock facts

- Softer coastal rocks erode quickly to form inwardly curved areas called bays.
- Harder rocks resist erosion for longer, creating headlands that jut out into the sea.
- Eroded coastal rocks sometimes leave behind stumps: small rock islands that may be submerged at high tide.
- A shingle beach is made of rock that has been eroded into pebble-sized pieces.
- As the shingle is eroded further by the waves, it eventually becomes sand.

Shingle erodes to form sand.

Did you know?

Golden sands are mainly quartz, white sands are mostly limestone, and black sands are rich in fragments of volcanic rocks such as basalt or obsidian.

Sand color

Using the information on this page to help you, label each photograph below to describe the type of sand.

Choose from:
volcanic sand   quartz-rich sand   limestone sand

1. ....

2. ....

3. ....

Metamorphism

Metamorphism is a process involving changes in pressure and/or heat in which the elements in a rock recombine to form new minerals and an entirely different rock structure. Metamorphism is usually a very slow process.

Types of metamorphism

Read each caption, then number the box beside it to match the correct section of the diagram.

Regional metamorphism affects large areas of rock buried deep within Earth's crust. The huge weight of rock above creates extreme pressure and increased heat.

Structural (or dynamic) metamorphism is caused by pressure exerted by movements of Earth's crust, either at boundaries between tectonic plates or on fractures within the plates known as faults.

Contact (or thermal) metamorphism occurs when magma breaks into existing rock structures and "bakes" the surrounding rocks.

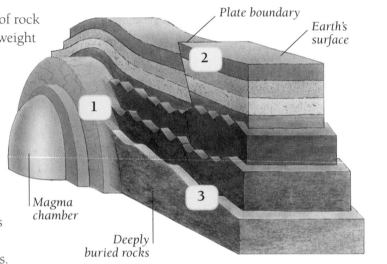

Plate boundary

Earth's surface

Magma chamber

Deeply buried rocks

Name the metamorphic rocks

Use the information in the table below and on page 8 to help you label each metamorphic rock with its name.

rock	texture	grain size	colors/patterns
green marble	granular	fine to coarse	a light-colored rock with uneven streaks of green
hornfels	foliated	fine	fine bands of color in a range of grays
gneiss	foliated	medium to coarse	light and dark bands, often folded (wavy)
slate	foliated	fine	uniform color; medium to dark gray

1. ....

2. ....

3. ....

4. ....

Rock Story

Most of what scientists know about the history of Earth comes from studying rocks and minerals. Sedimentary rocks are particularly valuable, providing evidence of many different types of events, including tectonic plate movements, climate changes, and natural disasters such as volcanic eruptions, floods, and meteorite impacts.

Rock story facts

- Scientists study pollen grains fossilized in rock to see which plants were growing when that rock was laid down. Different plants grow in different climates, so fossilized pollen gives clues about what the climate was like.

- Rocks also record global climate changes caused by violent volcanic eruptions and meteorite impacts.

- A mass extinction causes a sudden decrease in the number of species in the fossil record. There have been at least five such events in the past 450 million years.

- Scientists figure out the age of rocks using radiometric dating. Radioactive atoms in rocks decay at known rates. By measuring the numbers of these atoms present in a rock, scientists can calculate its age.

Rock story puzzle

Circle the correct word or phrase to complete each sentence.
Use the information on this page to help you.

1. The type of rocks that tell scientists most about the history of Earth are **igneous / sedimentary / metamorphic.**

2. Variations in climate are shown by the type of **radioactive atoms / fossilized pollen grains / minerals** a rock contains.

3. Scientists use **radiometric dating / microscopes / fossilized pollen grains** to figure out how old rocks are.

4. There have been at least **5 / 10 / 50** mass extinctions in the last 450 million years.

Flood!

Read the passage on the right, then fill in the missing words.
Choose from:

quartz   silt   conifer   remains   decay   water

A fossilized log from Petrified Forest National Park

1. About 225 million years ago the state of Arizona was covered in a forest of huge .... trees.

2. Fast-flowing .... from a sudden flood flattened the trees.

3. When the floodwaters receded, the trees were covered in vast amounts of ....

4. This slowed down the process of ....

5. Over many thousands of years, mineral-rich water soaked through the trees' cells, gradually replacing plant matter with .... crystals.

6. The .... of the ancient forest can be seen at Petrified Forest National Park. "Petrified" means "turned to stone."

Famous Rock Formations

Throughout the world there are natural rock formations that are so remarkable that they have become famous. Often they are notable because of their impressive size, distinctive shape, or some other unique feature. This page describes five famous rock formations from around the world, all of which are popular tourist destinations.

Yunnan Stone Forest, China

Where in the world?

Look at the pictures below. Using the descriptions, identify each rock formation, and write its name on the line.

1. The **Giant's Causeway** in Northern Ireland is a "pavement" of interlocking basalt columns, mainly hexagonal in shape, that formed tens of millions of years ago when basaltic lava cooled rapidly.

2. The **Grand Canyon** in Arizona is an enormous gorge, carved out of sandstone and limestone rock by the Colorado River during the last five or six million years.

3. **Uluru/Ayers Rock** is a large rock formation in Australia's Northern Territory. It is made of a coarse-grained type of sandstone called arkose. Iron-rich minerals on its surface produce a rusty orange color.

4. **Mont Saint-Michel** in Normandy, France, is a tidal island, surrounded by water only at high tide. It is a granite block that has resisted erosion from the sea longer than the softer surrounding rocks.

5. **Monument Valley** is north-east of the Grand Canyon, along the border between Utah and Arizona. The rock formations are formed by erosion—originally by water, and later by wind.

a. ....

b. ....

c. ....
....

d. ....

e. ....

Limestone Landscapes

Calcite, the main ingredient of limestone, dissolves in rainwater. When limestone becomes exposed on Earth's surface, rainwater seeps into tiny fractures in the rock and begins to dissolve it. Over time, these fractures enlarge, creating distinctive features such as limestone pavements. In many limestone areas, water working its way underground has carved out large cave systems.

True or false?

Using the information on this page, check the boxes to show which of these statements are true and which are false.

	TRUE	FALSE
1. Limestone rock is made mostly of the mineral calcite.	☐	☐
2. Stalactites and stalagmites grow by a few millimeters every day.	☐	☐
3. Stalagmites grow down from the roof of a cave.	☐	☐
4. Stalactites grow up from the floor of a cave.	☐	☐
5. Limestone caves are created by the action of water.	☐	☐

Cave facts

- When calcite-rich water drips through the roof of a limestone cave, some of it evaporates, leaving behind calcite deposits on the cave roof. These gradually grow downward to form stalactites.
- A stalagmite is created by calcite-rich water dripping onto the floor of a cave. A stalagmite grows upward.
- Stalactites and stalagmites grow slowly—by up to a few millimeters each year.
- Dripping water from stalactites often causes stalagmites to grow underneath them. Eventually, stalactites and stalagmites can grow together, forming pillars.

Grow your own stalactite

! **WARNING** Always wear gloves and goggles whenever you handle the Epsom salts.

Try this experiment to see for yourself how stalactites and stalagmites grow.

You need: • *gloves and goggles* • *2 cups of Epsom salts* • *2 cupfuls of hot water* • *large jug* • *mixing stick* • *2 glass jars* • *2 paper clips* • *saucer* • *about 12 in (30 cm) of wool yarn or cotton string*

1 Pour the Epsom salts and hot water into the jug. Stir with the mixing stick for several minutes until no more Epsom salts dissolve.

2 Pour the solution into the jars. Dunk the string in a jar and then run it between your fingers to remove any excess liquid. Attach paper clips to each end, and place one in each jar. Place the jars so the string sags in the middle. Put the saucer underneath to catch the drips.

3 After an hour, a drip of liquid should have formed where the string sags. If the string is dry, replace it with a more absorbent type of string or wool. If the saucer is full of liquid, replace the string with a less absorbent material.

4 Check the string daily to see how long the stalactite has become. How long is your stalactite after five days?

Mining and Quarrying

Mining is the process of extracting ore from the ground. If the ore lies deep below the surface, an underground mine is built. If it lies close to the surface, overlying soil and rock are removed, and the ore is accessed directly. This is known as surface mining. Surface mines that produce building materials are known as quarries.

A slate quarry in Wales

Mining facts

- The first stage in mining is mineral exploration—the search for ore deposits.

- Once an ore deposit is found, geologists estimate its size, quality, and possible value.

- If the estimated value of an ore deposit is greater than the cost of extracting it, then a mine may be built.

- When a mine is built, access roads are constructed, mine tunnels are dug, and mining equipment is installed for extracting the ore.

- After a mine shuts down, the land is reclaimed. It is cleaned up, made safe, and used for something else, such as real estate, an industrial or retail development, a wildlife preserve, or a public park. Surface mines may be filled with water to create lakes, or used as garbage dumps and landfill sites.

Did you know?

The deepest mines in the world are the Mponeng and TauTona gold mines in South Africa, with mining operations around 2.5 miles (4 km) below ground.

Stages in mining and quarrying

Read the sentences below about the different stages in mining and quarrying. Write a number in each box to show the correct order. Use the information in the facts box to the left to help you.

☐ Once an ore deposit is found, estimate its size and quality, and then calculate its possible value.

☐ Reclaim the land.

☐ Compare the possible value of the deposit with the cost of mining it to decide whether it is worth mining.

☐ Conduct mineral exploration.

☐ Mine the ore.

☐ If the deposit is worth mining, build access roads, dig the mine tunnels, and install the equipment.

Reclaiming the land

Look at the surface mine on the right. In the box below, draw a picture showing how the land could be used after the mine is abandoned. Use the information in the facts box to help you.

Rocks as Tools

Early hunter-gatherers used rocks to make axes, clubs, and spears for hunting, daggers for skinning carcasses and slicing meat, and adzes for building shelters. With the development of agriculture, new stone tools were invented, such as sickles for harvesting crops, querns for grinding grain, and spindle whorls for spinning wool.

Flint

Rock tools

Read each caption below, then number it to match the correct picture.

- [ ] Ancient Egyptian holding an adze, which was used to carve wooden objects.
- [ ] A stone quern (grinding stone), used for grinding grains to make flour.
- [ ] Two flint daggers from the European Beaker period (around 2800–1900 BCE).
- [ ] A flint arrowhead, at least 4,000 years old.
- [ ] Wool on a spindle, weighted with a stone spindle whorl.
- [ ] An adze. The flint adze head slots into a hollow piece of antler and both are strapped to the wooden handle with a leather thong.

Flint facts

- Many early tools were made of flint.
- Flint is a form of chalcedony, which is a type of quartz.
- Flint is found mainly in sedimentary rocks, such as limestone and chalk.
- Archaeologists have found flint tools in Ethiopia dating back 2.6 million years.
- Flint is ideal for making tools because it is easy to find, can be split in any direction, and forms a sharp edge.

Fascinating flint

Complete these facts by circling the right answers. Use the information from this page to help you.

1. Flint is a type of **feldspar / quartz / basalt**.
2. Flint is good for making sharp tools because it **is easy to find / is found in sedimentary rock / forms a sharp edge**.
3. Flint can be found in **limestone / granite / marble**.
4. The earliest known flint tools, dating back 2.6 million years, were found in **Egypt / Ethiopia / Europe**.

Building Stones

Rocks have been used as building materials since the beginning of civilization. Rock used in construction is referred to as stone. Stone lasts much longer than other building materials commonly used by our ancestors, such as wood or earth. Most old buildings that are still standing today are made of stone.

Building stones

Read each caption, then number the box beside it to match the correct picture.

☐ Granite is a natural stone that ranges in color from pink to gray to black. Because it is so hardwearing it is often used to make flooring and steps for public places.

☐ Brick is a manufactured building stone. Most bricks are made from clay and used for walls and paving.

☐ Concrete is made by mixing cement with sand, gravel, and water. When reinforced with steel bars, concrete is extremely strong and can be used to build very large structures.

☐ Another natural stone used for building is slate. Because it splits into regular flat sheets, it is ideal for use as a roofing material.

1

2

3

4

Famous stone structures

Look at the pictures of four famous stone structures, then read the descriptions underneath. Can you match the caption to the correct picture?

1.

2.

3.

4.

a. Stonehenge, an ancient stone circle in Wiltshire, England, is made from blocks of sandstone and a type of dolerite known as bluestone.

b. The Taj Mahal in Agra, India, is a tomb complex whose main building, the domed mausoleum, is made of white marble.

c. The Pyramids, in Egypt, were originally encased in a layer of polished white limestone. A few remains of the casing can be seen at the top of Khafre's pyramid (in the foreground).

d. The Great Wall of China was built from various materials, including granite, brick, wood, and earth.

Coal

Coal is formed from the remains of plants that grew in swamps hundreds of millions of years ago. Worldwide, coal is the largest single source of fuel for generating electricity. It is also used for powering furnaces, such as those used in the production of iron and steel.

The history of coal use

Read these captions about the history of coal use. Looking at the pictures for clues, fill in the missing words. Choose from:

fires   children   electricity   metal   steam engine

1. Since ancient times coal fires have been used to heat .... to make it easier to shape.

2. During the Industrial Revolution coal mining boomed, due to the invention of the coal-fired ....

3. At this time many .... were sent to work down in the coal mines.

4. In many parts of the world, coal .... were used for home heating and cooking until relatively recently.

5. Coal is still used throughout the world for generating ....

Coal story

Add arrows to show step by step how plant remains become coal. Use the information in the facts box on this page to help you.

Lignite

Anthracite

Dead plants

Bituminous coal

Peat

Coal facts

- When dead plants fall into a swamp, the pressure of over-lying layers changes them into peat, a wet, brown material.

- When peat is compressed it forms a dry, crumbly substance called lignite.

- Under pressure, lignite becomes bituminous coal, which is dull black with shiny patches.

- Extreme pressure over millions of years can transform bituminous coal into anthracite, which is hard and shiny.

Gemstones

Certain minerals known as gemstones are prized for their beauty and rarity. Their intense color and sparkle, together with their hardness and resistance to wear, make them highly sought-after for jewelry and for decorating artifacts. The most valuable gemstones are called precious. Other gemstones are described as semiprecious.

Gem facts

- Diamond is the hardest known natural mineral, made of pure crystals of carbon.
- The mineral corundum has several varieties. Tiny amounts of chromium create the red color of ruby. The blue of sapphire is caused by traces of iron and titanium.
- Beryl is another mineral with several gemstone forms. Emeralds are green and aquamarines are light blue.
- Topaz is found in many colors, including colorless, blue, green, pink, brown, and yellow.
- The principal color of opal may be clear, white, gray, or black. The iridescent colored patterns are created when light is scattered by minute spheres of silica inside the stone.

Precious gem colors

Color the gems below using appropriate colors. Use the information on this page to help you.

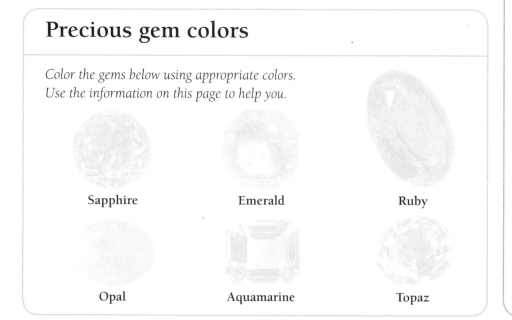

Sapphire   Emerald   Ruby

Opal   Aquamarine   Topaz

Semiprecious gemstones

Use the information below to label these photographs of semiprecious stones.

- **Agate** is a type of quartz found mainly in metamorphic rock. Banded agate is the type most commonly used as a gemstone.
- **Lapis lazuli**, a rock composed mainly of the mineral lazurite, is an intense, deep blue color.
- The term **jade** is used to describe the green varieties of two different minerals—jadeite and nephrite. Jade is semitransparent to opaque and a rich, green color.
- **Turquoise**, used in jewelry from the earliest times, is an opaque stone with a pale greenish-blue color.

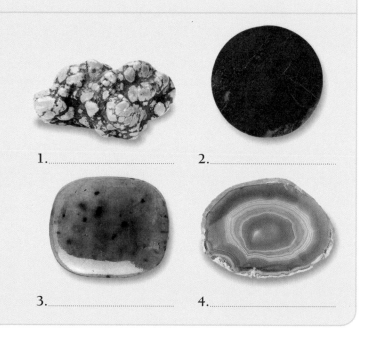

1. ....   2. ....

3. ....   4. ....

Metals

There are several stages in the production of metal from metal ore. First, the ore is crushed, and then its constituent minerals are separated from one another. The raw metal is then extracted from the metallic mineral in a process called reduction. Processing techniques vary, depending on the type of ore.

All sorts of metals

Complete the table below, using the information on page 11 to help you. Write the correct word on each dotted line, and draw the missing pictures for examples of how the metal is used. Choose from:

cassiterite   nickel   copper   bauxite
zinc   galena   cinnabar   iron

Name of metal	Principal ore	Properties	Uses	
1.	hematite	magnetic, brittle, corrodes easily	making steel, hulls of ships, railings	
aluminum	2.	lightweight, good electrical conductor, resists corrosion	power lines, aircraft, drink cans	
3.	chalcopyrite	soft, easily shaped, good electrical conductor	electrical wiring, water pipes	
4.	sphalerite	soft, easily shaped, resists corrosion	used to "galvanize" other metals—give them a coating to prevent corrosion	
tin	5.	low melting point, resistant to corrosion, good electrical conductor	solder (wire for making joints in metal), bronze, tinplating	
lead	6.	very soft, very dense, poisonous	car batteries, roofing, radiation shielding	
7.	nickeline	hard, highly resistant to corrosion, magnetic	magnets, batteries, coins	
mercury	8.	very dense, liquid at room temperature, poisonous	thermometers, compact fluorescent light bulb, dental fillings	

Precious Metals

Gold and silver were among the earliest metals discovered and have been valued through the ages for their beauty and rarity. Today gold is used for electrical contacts, silver is used to make photographic film, and platinum is used in car exhaust systems. All three are also used to make jewelry.

Did you know?

Aluminum was more valuable than gold until 1886, when a process was invented for extracting the metal from its ores.

Identify the mineral

Can you name these minerals? Use the information in the facts box to help you. Choose from:

silver   pyrite   gold   platinum

1. ....

2. ....

3. ....

4. ....

Precious metal facts

- Gold is a rich, yellow color. It is found as grains, nuggets, and as veins in quartz.

- Silver is a shiny white metal. It occurs as a native metal in dendrites (branching forms) and nuggets, and is also found in a variety of ores.

- Platinum is grayer than silver. It is found as grains, nuggets, and (more rarely) crystals.

- The mineral pyrite is known as "fool's gold" because novices sometimes mistake it for gold. Pyrite is not as yellow as gold.

Gold, silver, and platinum

Complete these facts by circling the right answers. Use information from this page and on the charts at the back of the book to help you.

1. **Gold / silver / platinum** is used in car exhaust systems.

2. Gold can be found as nuggets, grains, and **dendrites / crystals / veins**.

3. The mineral pyrite is known as **fool's gold / fool's silver / fool's platinum**.

4. **Silver / aluminum / pyrite** was once more valuable than gold.

5. The largest platinum nugget was discovered in **1843 / 1812 / 1869**.

6. The largest gold nugget ever found weighed **22 oz (621 g) / 156 lb (70.9 kg) / 22 lb (9.7 kg)**.

Other Uses for Rocks and Minerals

We have already seen how rocks and minerals are used for making tools, buildings, and jewelry, for generating electricity, as a source of metal, and as a store of value, but they have countless other uses. The majority of materials used in manufacturing originate from rocks and minerals.

Match it up

Draw lines to match the mineral on the left to one of its uses on the right. Use the information in the facts box to help you.

Clay

Talc

Gypsum

Rutile

Quartz

Petroleum

Mineral facts

- Clay is used to make pottery and tiles.
- The liquid petroleum is used to manufacture vehicle fuels and plastics.
- Soapstone rock is mostly made of talc, the softest naturally occurring mineral, and is easily carved into ornaments.
- Quartz sand is used in glass making and electronics.
- Gypsum is a very soft mineral, used to make plaster and chalkboard "chalk."
- The mineral rutile is used to make paint and sunscreen.

Which mineral?

Answer the questions below, using the information on this page to help you. Choose from:

**quartz   petroleum   talc
gypsum   rutile**

1. Which mineral is used in sunscreens? ....

2. Which mineral is used in electronics? ....

3. Which liquid mineral is used to manufacture vehicle fuels? ....

4. Which mineral is chalkboard "chalk" made from? ....

5. Which is the softest naturally occurring mineral? ....

Properties of Minerals

Minerals vary in many ways. Geologists find certain properties particularly useful when trying to identify an unknown mineral. These include its shape, its color, the way it reflects light and lets it through, the way it breaks, how easy it is to scratch, and how dense it is compared to water.

Types of luster

Read the descriptions of the different types of mineral luster, and then write the letter of the picture that illustrates it beside each one.

1. A **vitreous** luster is glassy. It is found most commonly in clear and semitransparent gemstones.

2. A **metallic** luster is shiny all over. All native metals have a metallic luster when newly broken or polished. It is also a feature of some ores and some nonmetals.

3. A mineral with a **submetallic** luster is shiny in places. Many metallic ores have a submetallic luster.

4. A **greasy** luster describes an oily appearance. Minerals with a greasy luster include halite, quartz, and apatite.

5. A **silky** luster is shimmery like silk. This is created by a fine structure of mineral fibers. Examples include wavellite, fibrous calcite, and tremolite.

a.

An aggregate of silver and copper

b.

Halite

c.

Tremolite

d.

Ruby

e.

Lepidocrocite

Mineral facts

- A mineral's shape is described by its crystal system and habit.
- How a mineral reflects light is known as its luster.
- Clarity describes how much light a mineral lets through.
- A mineral has cleavage if it breaks along well-defined planes of weakness.
- A mineral is said to fracture if it breaks unevenly.
- Hardness measures how easily a mineral can be scratched.

Mohs' scale

On this scale, which measures the hardness of minerals, each mineral scratches only those below it.

HARDEST

10		Diamond
9		Corundum
8		Topaz
7		Quartz
6		Orthoclase
5		Apatite
4		Fluorite
3		Calcite
2		Gypsum
1		Talc

SOFTEST

Hardness test

Use this scratch test to compare the hardness of rocks and minerals.

You need:
- *6 specimens of rocks or minerals*
- *scratching tools (e.g. copper coin, iron nail, penknife, steel file, sandpaper)*

! *Ask an adult to help you use the penknife, steel file, nail, and sandpaper.*

1 Write the names of the rocks or minerals whose hardness you are testing in the top row of the table below. For any mineral whose name you don't know, write a description or draw a sketch.

2 Try scratching each specimen with your fingernail, which has a hardness on Mohs' scale of 2.5. Anything it can scratch must have a lower hardness. Note your results in the table.

3 Try scratching any specimen that was not scratched by your fingernail with a copper coin, which has a hardness of 3.5, and any specimen not scratched by the coin with an iron nail, which has a hardness of 4.5.

4 With the help of an adult, try scratching the remaining unscratched specimens first with a penknife blade (hardness of 5.5), then a steel file (hardness of 6.5) and finally a piece of sandpaper (hardness of 7.5).

Rock or mineral (e.g. fluorite)						
Scratched by (e.g. iron nail)						
Hardness lower than (e.g. 4.5)						

Properties puzzle

Complete the sentences by circling the correct words or phrases. Use the information on these two pages to help you.

1. A mineral's hardness is a measure of how easily it can be **broken / scratched / bent**.

2. A mineral will scratch any mineral with a **lower / higher / equal** hardness on Mohs' scale.

3. How much light a mineral lets through is known as its **luster / clarity / cleavage**.

4. A mineral with a vitreous luster looks **oily / shiny / glassy**.

5. Very shiny minerals are described as having a **greasy / metallic / silky luster**.

Did you know?

When viewed under ultraviolet light, certain minerals glow. This property, called fluorescence, gets is name from the mineral fluorite.

Fluorite glows bright blue in ultraviolet light

Cutting and Polishing

Since ancient times people have been cutting and polishing stones to make them look more attractive. Cutting and polishing stones alters their optical properties to improve their color, clarity, and luster.

Gem cuts

- Flat faces on gemstones are called facets. A table cut has a single central facet at the top (called the "table") surrounded by a single facet on each side. Table cuts are usually square or rectangular in outline.

- The cabochon, a popular cut for opaque stones, has a smooth, curved surface. The most common shape for cabochons is an oval.

- A rose cut has many triangular facets. It is usually circular or oval in outline.

- A step cut has an outline that is a square, a rectangle, or a truncated rectangle (a rectangle with its corners cut off). There is a large central table and the other facets form a series of "steps" around it.

- A brilliant cut has many facets in various shapes at a variety of angles. Brilliant cuts are used most frequently when cutting diamonds and other colorless gems. The two most common outline shapes are round and pear (teardrop shape).

Which cut?

Look at the pictures of cut gemstones below. Use the information on this page to identify the cut of each stone, and then write the type of cut on the dotted line.

Choose from:

table cut	cabochon
rose cut	step cut
pear brilliant	round brilliant

Garnet

1. ....

Rose quartz

2. ....

Epidote

3. ....

Morganite

4. ....

Jet

5. ....

Labradorite

6. ....

Collecting Rocks

If you enjoy learning about rocks and minerals, you might want to start your own collection. To find out which are the best places to hunt for rocks and minerals in your local area, join a geology club or ask for information at your local library or museum.

Useful rock-collecting equipment: backpack, hammer, safety goggles, map, compass, whistle, pencils, notebook, and bubble wrap for protecting your finds.

Collecting samples

Read the sentences carefully and then number them from 1 to 5 to show their correct order.

☐ **a.** If you decide to take a specimen home, wrap it up in bubble wrap to protect it on the journey.

☐ **b.** Remove your chosen rock or mineral specimen carefully.

☐ **c.** When you have identified your specimen, label it and store it carefully.

☐ **d.** When you get home, unpack your specimen, clean it, and then identify it.

☐ **e.** When you find an interesting rock or mineral make a sketch of its location or take a picture.

Starting a collection

You need:
- *white correction fluid*
- *permanent marker (fine tip)*
- *cotton balls or tissue paper*
- *index card file*
- *cardboard specimen trays*

1 When you have identified your specimens put a small dab of correction fluid on the bottom of each one and let it dry. Use the permanent marker to write a reference number on each dab of correction fluid, starting with 1.

2 Fill out an index card for each specimen, writing its number at the top of the card. Include as much information as you can about the specimen—for example, location found, date found, weight, photo or sketch (if taken)—and the results of any tests you have carried out on it (see pages 31, 34, and 35).

3 Place each specimen in a cardboard tray, putting cotton balls or tissue paper underneath for protection.

Collecting tips

- Never go rock collecting alone. Always take an adult.
- Avoid quarries, cliffs, and rubbly slopes; they can be very dangerous.
- Don't take rocks from protected areas.
- Seek permission before entering private land.
- Wherever possible, collect loose rocks rather than hammering outcrops.
- A hammer should only be used by an adult and safety goggles should be worn.
- Never take rocks from walls, bridges, or buildings.
- Beaches, riverbanks, and gardens are good places to look for rocks.

Identifying Specimens

If you do a lot of collecting it may be worth buying an identification guide. A good identification guide will display a color photo of each rock or mineral and list several of its properties. The tests on these pages will help you discover some of a specimen's properties, which in turn will help you to identify it.

Specific gravity test

Try this test to find out the specific gravity of your rock and mineral specimens.

You need:
- *kitchen scale*
- *jug*
- *large bowl*
- *rock or mineral specimen*

1 Weigh your specimen and make a note of its weight.

2 Place the jug inside the bowl. Fill the jug with water to the brim, taking care not to spill any into the bowl.

3 Place the specimen gently into the water and let go. The volume of water displaced into the bowl will equal the volume of the specimen.

4 Carefully remove the jug from the bowl, making sure not to spill any more water into the bowl.

5 Weigh the water in the bowl and make a note of its weight. Use the same units as you used to weigh your specimen. For example, if you weighed the specimen in grams, weigh the water in grams, too.

6 Calculate the specific gravity of your specimen by dividing the weight of your specimen by the weight of the equal volume of water.

What is the specific gravity of the following specimens?
Complete the table. A calculator may be useful.

Choose from: 5.3   2.1   4.5   3.6

Specimen	Weight of specimen	Weight of water displaced	Specific gravity
A	105 g	50 g	....
B	108 g	30 g	....
C	144 g	32 g	....
D	106 g	20 g	....

Identification

- You may be able to identify some specimens simply by looking at them and noting their shape, color, luster, and clarity (see page 30).
- Be careful when identifying a mineral by color, because chemical impurities may have altered its color. To find its true color, do a **streak test** (see page 35).
- If a mineral breaks to leave surfaces that are uneven, it is said to **fracture**. Different minerals create different fracture patterns (see page 35).
- Calculating a specimen's **specific gravity** (see left) can also help you identify it.
- Another way of identifying rocks and minerals is by their **hardness** (see pages 30–31).

True or false?

Using the information on this page, check the boxes to show which of these facts are true and which are false.

	TRUE	FALSE
1. A specimen's specific gravity is its weight in relation to the weight of the same volume of water.	☐	☐
2. A mineral's color can be altered by chemical impurities.	☐	☐
3. A mineral is said to fracture if it breaks to leave surfaces that are even.	☐	☐
4. A streak test can help you discover a mineral's fracture pattern.	☐	☐

Fracture types

Can you figure out which fracture type each of these minerals has? Write a number in each of the boxes to match the types of fracture listed below.

1. Copper has a **jagged** fracture pattern with sharp, uneven edges.
2. Flint fractures in a **conchoidal** (smoothly curved) pattern.
3. The pink mineral petalite has a **subconchoidal**, smooth but less curved fracture pattern.
4. Wollastonite is an off-white mineral with a **splintery** fracture pattern.
5. Sillimanite is a brown mineral with an **uneven** fracture.

Petalite

Copper

Flint

Sillimanite

Wollastonite

Streak test

Try out this streak test to help you identify your mineral specimens. This test only works for minerals; it does not work for rocks.

You need:
- selection of minerals (e.g. hematite, iron pyrite, quartz, calcite, azurite, and chalcopyrite)
- porcelain tiles with white, unglazed backs

1 Scratch the mineral along the back of a tile to make a streak.

2 You can look up the streak color of any mineral in a field guide. Here are the streak colors of the minerals listed above:

hematite: dark red **calcite**: white
iron pyrite: greenish-black **azurite**: pale blue
quartz: white **chalcopyrite**: dark green.

3 If the mineral is too hard to make a streak, ask an adult to crush a small amount with a hammer. The color of the mineral's powder is the same as its streak color.

Geological Timeline

From studying rocks and fossils, geologists and paleontologists have built up a history of Earth. They have divided the time since the formation of Earth into thirteen parts called periods, illustrated in the timeline below. "Mya" is an abbreviation for millions of years ago.

Complete the timeline

Use page 12 and the charts at the back of the book to fill in the missing information on this timeline. Then draw in the missing pictures.

Meteor strike

(145–65 mya)
Flowering plants and small mammals appear. Dinosaurs become extinct at the end of this period, perhaps wiped out by a massive
....

Cambrian
(541–485 mya)
A wide range of marine life suddenly appears, known as the Cambrian Explosion.

Ordovician
(485–443 mya)
The first fish appear in shallow seas. The first simple plants appear on land.

Start here *and follow the timeline in a counterclockwise direction.*

Pre-Cambrian
(4,600–541 mya)
Simple plants and animals evolve. The world's oldest rock, the ....
in Canada, dates from the Pre-Cambrian period.

Silurian
(433–419 mya)
Oxygen-forming plants appear on land.

Devonian
(419–359 mya)
The seas are full of fish. Some fish evolve to walk on land.

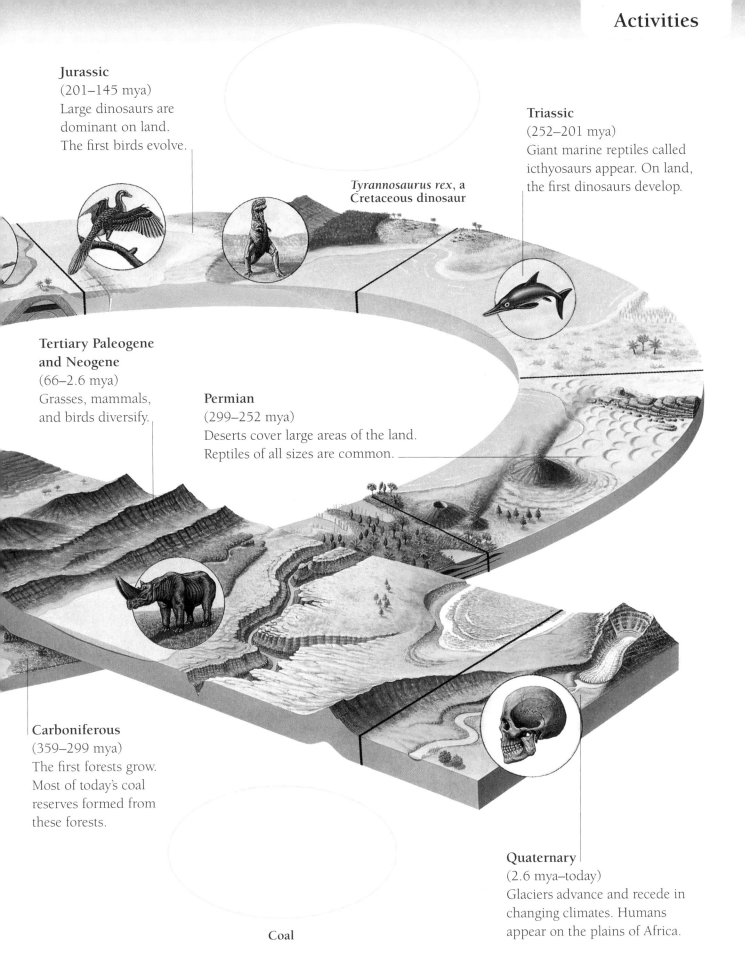

Jurassic
(201–145 mya)
Large dinosaurs are
dominant on land.
The first birds evolve.

Tyrannosaurus rex, a
Cretaceous dinosaur

Triassic
(252–201 mya)
Giant marine reptiles called
icthyosaurs appear. On land,
the first dinosaurs develop.

**Tertiary Paleogene
and Neogene**
(66–2.6 mya)
Grasses, mammals,
and birds diversify.

Permian
(299–252 mya)
Deserts cover large areas of the land.
Reptiles of all sizes are common.

Carboniferous
(359–299 mya)
The first forests grow.
Most of today's coal
reserves formed from
these forests.

Coal

Quaternary
(2.6 mya–today)
Glaciers advance and recede in
changing climates. Humans
appear on the plains of Africa.

37

Rocks

Check or number the boxes to answer each question. Check your answers on page 46.

1 A rock is a naturally occurring combination of:

- ☐ **a.** one or more elements
- ☐ **b.** two or more elements
- ☐ **c.** one or more minerals
- ☐ **d.** two or more minerals

2 About how far do tectonic plates move per year?

- ☐ **a.** between 0.2 and 2 inches (0.5 and 5 cm)
- ☐ **b.** between 0.4 and 6 inches (1 and 15 cm)
- ☐ **c.** between 2 and 20 inches (5 and 50 cm)

3 Rocks created as the result of volcanic activity are known as:

- ☐ **a.** sedimentary
- ☐ **b.** metamorphic
- ☐ **c.** igneous
- ☐ **d.** protoliths

4 Check all the characteristics of a shield volcano.

- ☐ **a.** runny magma
- ☐ **b.** thick magma
- ☐ **c.** effusive (nonexplosive) eruptions
- ☐ **d.** explosive eruptions
- ☐ **e.** gently sloping sides

5 Which famous rock formation was created by rapidly cooling lava?

- ☐ **a.** Giant's Causeway
- ☐ **b.** Grand Canyon
- ☐ **c.** Monument Valley
- ☐ **d.** Uluru/Ayers Rock

6 Rocks are brought to the surface as the result of volcanic activity. Number these captions 1 to 4 to show what happens next in the rock cycle.

- ☐ **a.** Rock fragments are transported by wind and water and deposited to form sediment.
- ☐ **b.** The process of metamorphism transforms rocks into new rocks.
- ☐ **c.** The process of lithification turns sediment into rock.
- ☐ **d.** The processes of weathering and erosion wear rocks down.

7 Which of the following processes is *not* part of weathering and erosion?

- ☐ **a.** abrasion
- ☐ **b.** corrosion
- ☐ **c.** freeze-thaw
- ☐ **d.** lithification

8 What is the name for the sediment carried by a river?

- ☐ **a.** its suspension
- ☐ **b.** its solution
- ☐ **c.** its load
- ☐ **d.** its deposition

9 Contact metamorphism is caused by:

- ☐ **a.** movement of tectonic plates
- ☐ **b.** magma baking the surrounding rocks
- ☐ **c.** a high velocity meteor impact

10 The Moon does not have a rock cycle because it has:

- ☐ **a.** no atmosphere and no tectonic plates
- ☐ **b.** no atmosphere
- ☐ **c.** no tectonic plates
- ☐ **d.** no life

All Sorts of Fossils

Check or number the boxes to answer each question. Check your answers on page 46.

1 Which of these is *not* a true fossil?

- ☐ a. a fossilized leaf
- ☐ b. a fossilized footprint
- ☐ c. a fossilized log
- ☐ d. a fossilized skeleton

2 Most fossils are found in:

- ☐ a. igneous rocks
- ☐ b. metamorphic rocks
- ☐ c. sedimentary rocks
- ☐ d. extrusive rocks

3 Fossilized tree resin is called:

- ☐ a. jet
- ☐ b. amber
- ☐ c. coral
- ☐ d. pearl

4 The first dinosaurs evolved during which geological period?

- ☐ a. Permian
- ☐ b. Triassic
- ☐ c. Jurassic
- ☐ d. Cretaceous

5 The oldest fossils discovered are:

- ☐ a. several thousand years old
- ☐ b. several million years old
- ☐ c. several billion years old
- ☐ d. several trillion years old

6 Check all the things that are useful when you go hunting for fossils.

- ☐ a. map
- ☐ b. backpack
- ☐ c. compass
- ☐ d. pencils
- ☐ e. notebook

7 Number the stages 1 to 5 to show how a fossil is formed.

- ☐ a. Successive layers of sediment push the remains deeper.
- ☐ b. An animal or plant dies.
- ☐ c. Plate movements and erosion bring the fossil to the surface.
- ☐ d. The remains become fossilized.
- ☐ e. Sediments bury the remains before they can decay.

8 What type of fossil gives clues about the type of climate when the rock was laid down?

- ☐ a. fossilized droppings
- ☐ b. fossilized bacteria
- ☐ c. fossilized pollen grains
- ☐ d. fossilized bones

9 *Tyrannosaurus rex* was the dominant land predator during which geological period?

- ☐ a. Permian
- ☐ b. Triassic
- ☐ c. Jurassic
- ☐ d. Cretaceous

10 The sudden appearance of a wide range of marine life about 550 million years ago is known as the:

- ☐ a. Cambrian Explosion
- ☐ b. Ordovician Explosion
- ☐ c. Silurian Explosion
- ☐ d. Devonian Explosion

Using Rocks and Minerals

Check or number the boxes to answer each question. Check your answers on page 46.

1 Humans have been using rocks as tools for at least:

- ☐ **a.** 26,000 years
- ☐ **b.** 260,000 years
- ☐ **c.** 2.6 million years
- ☐ **d.** 26 million years

2 A quarry is:

- ☐ **a.** any surface mine
- ☐ **b.** a surface mine that produces building materials
- ☐ **c.** any underground mine
- ☐ **d.** an underground mine that produces metal

3 Which two ingredients are *not* used to make concrete?

- ☐ **a.** cement
- ☐ **b.** gravel
- ☐ **c.** gypsum
- ☐ **d.** clay
- ☐ **e.** sand

4 Check all the famous structures that are made of stone.

- ☐ **a.** Eiffel Tower
- ☐ **b.** Taj Mahal
- ☐ **c.** Pyramids of Giza
- ☐ **d.** Golden Gate Bridge
- ☐ **e.** Stonehenge

5 Number the stages 1 to 5 to show how coal is formed.

- ☐ **a.** lignite
- ☐ **b.** anthracite
- ☐ **c.** dead plants
- ☐ **d.** bituminous coal
- ☐ **e.** peat

6 Today, the main use of coal worldwide is for:

- ☐ **a.** powering engines
- ☐ **b.** heating homes
- ☐ **c.** drying grain
- ☐ **d.** generating electricity

7 Which mineral is chalkboard chalk made from?

- ☐ **a.** talc
- ☐ **b.** chalk
- ☐ **c.** gypsum
- ☐ **d.** clay

8 Pottery and tiles are made from which mineral?

- ☐ **a.** rutile
- ☐ **b.** gypsum
- ☐ **c.** quartz
- ☐ **d.** clay

9 Plastics are made from:

- ☐ **a.** coal
- ☐ **b.** petroleum
- ☐ **c.** rutile
- ☐ **d.** quartz

10 Which mineral is used to make glass?

- ☐ **a.** clay
- ☐ **b.** rutile
- ☐ **c.** quartz
- ☐ **d.** talc

11 Which mineral is used to make sunscreens and paints?

- ☐ **a.** rutile
- ☐ **b.** petroleum
- ☐ **c.** clay
- ☐ **d.** quartz

Describing Minerals

Check or number the boxes to answer each question. Check your answers on page 46.

1 Which is the largest class of rock-forming minerals?

- ☐ a. carbonate minerals
- ☐ b. oxide minerals
- ☐ c. silicate minerals
- ☐ d. sulphate minerals

2 When two or more crystals intersect it is known as:

- ☐ a. crossing
- ☐ b. doubling
- ☐ c. pairing
- ☐ d. twinning

3 Which is *not* a crystal habit?

- ☐ a. acicular
- ☐ b. cubic
- ☐ c. dendritic
- ☐ d. botryoidal

4 The property of how a mineral reflects light is known as its:

- ☐ a. cleavage
- ☐ b. clarity
- ☐ c. purity
- ☐ d. luster

5 The hardness of minerals is measured using:

- ☐ a. Mohs' Scale
- ☐ b. Ohm's Scale
- ☐ c. The Mineral Hardness Scale
- ☐ d. The Richter Scale

6 Number the stages 1 to 4 to show how to find a rock or mineral's specific gravity.

- ☐ a. Weigh the water displaced by the specimen.
- ☐ b. Weigh the specimen.
- ☐ c. Divide the weight of the specimen by the weight of the water it displaced.
- ☐ d. Place the specimen in a full jug of water.

7 A mineral that looks oily has a:

- ☐ a. submetallic luster
- ☐ b. metallic luster
- ☐ c. greasy luster
- ☐ d. vitreous luster

8 The water-soluble mineral that forms limestone landscapes is:

- ☐ a. dolomite
- ☐ b. calcite
- ☐ c. aragonite
- ☐ d. talc

9 The property that some minerals have of breaking along well-defined planes of weakness is known as:

- ☐ a. shear
- ☐ b. fracture
- ☐ c. cleavage
- ☐ d. habit

10 Check all the fracture patterns.

- ☐ a. splintery
- ☐ b. rough
- ☐ c. conchoidal
- ☐ d. jagged
- ☐ e. pretty

11 White sand is made mainly from:

- ☐ a. limestone
- ☐ b. obsidian
- ☐ c. basalt
- ☐ d. quartz

Metals and Ores

Check or number the boxes to answer each question. Check your answers on page 46.

1 The most abundant metal on Earth is:

- a. zinc
- b. silver
- c. copper
- d. aluminum

2 The most widely used metal is:

- a. lead
- b. gold
- c. iron
- d. tin

3 The principal ore of iron is:

- a. chalcopyrite
- b. bauxite
- c. galena
- d. hematite

4 Which metal ore is the most magnetic naturally occurring mineral on Earth?

- a. magnetite
- b. cassiterite
- c. nickelite
- d. cinnabar

5 What is an alloy?

- a. a precious metal
- b. a mixture that includes one or more metals
- c. a mixture that includes two or more metals
- d. a native metal

6 Check all the alloys.

- a. bronze
- b. brass
- c. steel
- d. nickel

7 Which of these metals is liquid at room temperature?

- a. zinc
- b. mercury
- c. lead
- d. copper

8 Number the stages of metal production from 1 to 4.

- a. Extract the raw metal from the metallic mineral.
- b. Crush the ore.
- c. Mine the ore.
- d. Separate the minerals in the ore from one another.

9 Which mineral is known as "fool's gold"?

- a. cassiterite
- b. sphalerite
- c. bauxite
- d. pyrite

10 Which of these metals is *not* precious?

- a. aluminum
- b. platinum
- c. gold
- d. silver

Gemstones

Check or number the boxes to answer each question. Check your answers on page 46.

1 What is diamond made of?

- ☐ **a.** phosphorous
- ☐ **b.** nitrogen
- ☐ **c.** carbon
- ☐ **d.** silicon

2 Which two gemstones are varieties of the mineral corundum?

- ☐ **a.** topaz
- ☐ **b.** sapphire
- ☐ **c.** opal
- ☐ **d.** jade
- ☐ **e.** ruby

3 Emeralds and aquamarines are varieties of which mineral?

- ☐ **a.** topaz
- ☐ **b.** corundum
- ☐ **c.** beryl
- ☐ **d.** agate

4 What color is lapis lazuli?

- ☐ **a.** deep blue
- ☐ **b.** green
- ☐ **c.** pale, greenish-blue
- ☐ **d.** red

5 Gemstones that are not precious are described as:

- ☐ **a.** cheap
- ☐ **b.** unprecious
- ☐ **c.** non-precious
- ☐ **d.** semiprecious

6 The gemstone agate is a variety of which mineral?

- ☐ **a.** quartz
- ☐ **b.** corundum
- ☐ **c.** beryl
- ☐ **d.** lazurite

7 Which word is *not* used to describe the cut of gemstones?

- ☐ **a.** step
- ☐ **b.** facet
- ☐ **c.** cabochon
- ☐ **d.** stair

8 People who cut and polish gems are known as:

- ☐ **a.** petrologists
- ☐ **b.** gemologists
- ☐ **c.** rockhounds
- ☐ **d.** lapidaries

9 Check all the gem cuts.

- ☐ **a.** table cut
- ☐ **b.** chair cut
- ☐ **c.** brilliant cut
- ☐ **d.** daisy cut
- ☐ **e.** rose cut

10 Jade is the green variety of jadeite and which other mineral?

- ☐ **a.** nephrite
- ☐ **b.** lazurite
- ☐ **c.** corundum
- ☐ **d.** beryl

Activity Answers

Once you have completed each page of activities, check your answers below.

Page 14
Inside a volcano
1 (strata) layers from previous eruptions
2 lava flow
3 magma chamber
4 ash cloud
5 eruption at central vent
6 eruption at side vent
7 conduit

Page 14
Identify the volcano
1 b   2 c   3 a

Page 15
What caused it?
1 a glacier
2 wave action
3 corrosion
4 wind-borne particles
5 freeze-thaw
6 flowing water

Page 15
Weathering and erosion puzzle
1 break rocks down
2 worn away
3 dissolved
4 a large
5 wind

Page 16
Fast water, slow water
In which jar did the most soil fall to the bottom? Jar 1.
The faster the water is moving, the **less** sediment is deposited.
The slower the water is moving, the **more** sediment is deposited.

Page 16
True or false?
1 True
2 False. Most of the sediment carried by a river is deposited near its mouth.
3 True
4 False. The faster water flows, the more sediment it can carry.
5 True

Page 17
Seashore rock formations
1 headland
2 cliffs
3 stumps
4 sand
5 boulder
6 bay
7 shingle

Page 17
Sand color
1 Limestone sand
2 Volcanic sand
3 Quartz-rich sand

Page 18
Types of metamorphism
1 Contact (or thermal) metamorphism
2 Structural (or dynamic) metamorphism
3 Regional metamorphism

Page 18
Name the metamorphic rocks
1 slate
2 hornfels
3 green marble
4 gneiss

Page 19
Rock story puzzle
1 sedimentary
2 fossilized pollen grains
3 radiometric dating
4 5

Page 19
Flood!
1 conifer
2 water
3 silt
4 decay
5 quartz
6 remains

Page 20
Where in the world?
1 b
2 d
3 c
4 e
5 a

Page 21
True or false?
1 True
2 False. Stalactites and stalagmites grow by a few millimeters every year.
3 False. Stalagmites grow up from the floor of a cave.
4 False. Stalactites grow down from the roof of a cave.
5 True

Page 22
Stages in mining and quarrying
1 Conduct mineral exploration.
2 Once an ore deposit is found, estimate its size and quality and calculate its possible value.
3 Compare the possible value of the deposit with the cost of mining it to decide whether it is worth mining.
4 If the deposit is worth mining, build access roads, dig the mine tunnels, and install the equipment.
5 Mine the ore.
6 Reclaim the land.

Page 23
Rock tools
1 A flint arrowhead, at least 4,000 years old
2 An adze. The flint adze head is contained in an antler sleeve, and both are attached to the wooden handle with a leather thong.
3 Ancient Egyptian holding an adze, which was used to carve wooden objects
4 Two flint daggers from the European Beaker period (around 2800–900 BCE)
5 Wool on a spindle, weighted with a stone spindle whorl
6 A stone quern (grinding stone), used for grinding grains to make flour

Page 23
Fascinating flint
1 quartz
2 forms a sharp edge
3 limestone
4 Ethiopia

Page 24
Building stones
1 slate
2 concrete
3 granite
4 brick

Page 24
Famous stone structures
1 b   2 c   3 d   4 a

Page 25
The history of coal use
1 metal
2 steam engine
3 children
4 fires
5 electricity

Page 25
Coal story

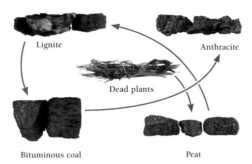

Lignite — Anthracite — Dead plants — Bituminous coal — Peat

Page 26
Gem colors
Sapphire blue
Emerald green
Ruby red
Opal clear, white, gray, or black background with multicolored patterns
Aquamarine light blue
Topaz colorless, blue, green, pink, brown, or yellow

Page 26
Semiprecious gemstones
1 turquoise
2 lapis lazuli
3 jade
4 agate

Page 27
All sorts of metals
1 iron
2 bauxite
3 copper
4 zinc
5 cassiterite
6 galena
7 nickel
8 cinnabar

Page 28
Identify the mineral
1 platinum
2 pyrite
3 silver
4 gold

Page 28
Gold, silver, and platinum
1 platinum
2 veins
3 fool's gold
4 aluminum
5 1843
6 156 lb (70.9 kg)

Page 29
Match it up

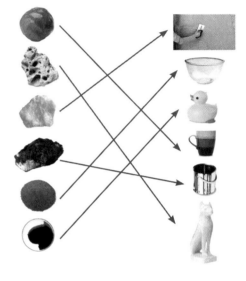

Page 29
Which mineral?
1 rutile
2 quartz
3 petroleum
4 gypsum
5 talc

Pages 30
Types of luster
1 d
2 a
3 e
4 b
5 c

Pages 31
Properties puzzle
1 scratched
2 lower
3 clarity
4 glassy
5 metallic

Page 32
Which cut?
1 step cut
2 round brilliant
3 table cut
4 pear brilliant
5 rose cut
6 cabochon

Page 33
Collecting samples
1 e 2 b 3 a
4 d 5 c

Page 34
Specific gravity test
A 2.1
B 3.6
C 4.5
D 5.3

Page 34
True or false?
1 True
2 True
3 False. A mineral is said to fracture if it breaks to leave surfaces that are uneven.
4 False. A streak test can help you discover a mineral's streak color.

Page 35
Fracture types
1 Copper
2 Flint
3 Petalite
4 Wollastonite
5 Sillimanite

Pages 36 to 37
Complete the timeline
Cretaceous **(145–66 mya)**
Flowering plants and small mammals appear. Dinosaurs become extinct at the end of this period, wiped out by a massive asteroid impact
Pre-Cambrian World's oldest rock: Acasta Gneiss

Quick Quiz Answers
Once you have completed each page of quiz questions, check your answers below.

Page 38
Rocks
1 c 2 b 3 c 4 a, c, e 5 a 6 a 2, b 4, c 3, d 1 7 d 8 c 9 b 10 a

Page 39
All sorts of fossils
1 b 2 c 3 b 4 b 5 c 6 a, b, c, d, e 7 a 3, b 1, c 5, d 4, e 2 8 c 9 d 10 a

Page 40
Using rocks and minerals
1 c 2 b 3 c, d 4 b, c, e 5 a 3, b 5, c 1, d 4, e 2 6 d 7 c 8 d 9 b 10 c 11 a

Page 41
Describing minerals
1 c 2 d 3 b 4 d 5 a 6 a 3, b 1, c 4, d 2 7 c 8 b 9 c 10 a, c, d 11 a

Page 42
Metals and ores
1 d 2 c 3 d 4 a 5 b 6 a, b, c 7 b 8 a 4, b 2, c 1, d 3 9 d 10 a

Page 43
Gemstones
1 c 2 b, e 3 c 4 a 5 d 6 a 7 d 8 d 9 a, c, e 10 a

Acknowledgments

The publisher would like to thank the following:

Julie Ferris for proofreading.
Robert Dinwiddie for 2020 consultant review.
Harish Aggarwal, Senior DTP Designer.
Priyanka Sharma, Jackets Editorial Coordinator.

The publisher would like to thank the following for their kind permission to reproduce their photographs:

(Key: a-above; b-below/bottom; c-center; f-far; l-left; r-right; t-top)

DK Images: 3 Natural History Museum, London (tr -liquid mercury) (bl). 6 Natural History Museum, London (clb -gold) (fcl). 8 Natural History Museum, London (fclb) (cra); Science Museum, London (clb -pumice). 9 Natural History Museum, London (cr -mica) (fcra). 10 Judith Miller / HY Duke and Son (fcra) (bc -acicular crystals); Natural History Museum, London (clb). 11 Natural History Museum, London (clb -hematite). 12 Natural History Museum, London (c -mudstone); Royal Tyrrell Museum of Palaeontology, Alberta, Canada (cra). 13 Natural History Museum, London (bl). **NASA:** 13 (c); JPL (ca -Apollo 12). **DK Images:** 17 Rough Guides (bc). 19 Rainbow Forest Museum, Arizona (bl). 20 Rough Guides (cr). 24 Jorn Bohmer-Olsen and Rolf Sorensen (fcra); Natural History Museum, London (tr); Rough Guides (br -sticker). 25 Emma Firth (cr -fire); Science Museum, London (c) (c -topaz) (cl -aquamarine). 26 Natural History Museum, London (fcl -opal) (fcrb). 27 Rough Guides (cra -sticker). 28 Natural History Museum, London (cr -mineral 3). 29 Natural History Museum, London (bl). 30 Natural History Museum, London (cr -diamond) (c) (cb). 31 Natural History Museum, London (br). 37 Senckenberg, Forschungsinstitut und Naturmuseum, Frankfurt (tl -sticker). **NASA:** 38 JPL (br). **DK Images:** 40 Rough Guides (bc). Natural History Museum, London (ca). 42 Natural History Museum, London (crb).

Jacket images: Front: DK Images: Natural History Museum, London bl, cr; Satellite Imagemap, ©1996-2003, Planetary Visions br. **Back: DK Images:** Natural History Museum, London clb, cr, tr. **Back Flap: DK Images:** National Trust br; Natural History Museum, London bl, crb (pumice), ftl, tl (obsidian); **NASA:** cl.

All other images © Dorling Kindersley
For further information see:
www.dkimages.com

ROCK FACTS

ROCK	GABBRO	BASALT	GRANITE
TYPE	IGNEOUS	IGNEOUS	IGNEOUS
COMPOSITION	PYROXENE, FELDSPAR, AMPHIBOLE, OLIVINE	FELDSPAR, PYROXENE, OLIVINE	FELDSPAR, QUARTZ, MICA
GRAIN SIZE	COARSE	FINE	COARSE
LOCATION	VOLCANIC REGIONS	VOLCANIC REGIONS	VOLCANIC REGIONS

ROCK	RHYOLITE	SCHIST	SLATE
TYPE	IGNEOUS	METAMORPHIC	METAMORPHIC
COMPOSITION	FELDSPAR, QUARTZ, MICA	LONG GRAINS OF VARIOUS MINERALS	QUARTZ WITH MUSCOVITE OR ILLITE
GRAIN SIZE	FINE	MEDIUM TO COARSE	FINE
LOCATION	VOLCANIC REGIONS	MOUNTAINS	MOUNTAINS

ROCK	GNEISS	MARBLE	BRECCIA
TYPE	METAMORPHIC	METAMORPHIC	SEDIMENTARY
COMPOSITION	QUARTZ, FELDSPAR, MICA	CALCITE	ANGULAR FRAGMENTS OF ROCKS AND MINERALS
GRAIN SIZE	MEDIUM TO COARSE	FINE TO COARSE	VERY COARSE
LOCATION	MOUNTAINS	VOLCANIC REGIONS	COASTS

ROCK	SANDSTONE	SHALE	LIMESTONE
TYPE	SEDIMENTARY	SEDIMENTARY	SEDIMENTARY
COMPOSITION	QUARTZ, FELDSPAR, MICA	CLAY MINERALS, QUARTZ, MICA, FELDSPAR	CALCITE
GRAIN SIZE	MEDIUM	FINE	COARSE TO FINE
LOCATION	INLAND, SEABEDS, FRESHWATER	SEABEDS	SEABEDS, FRESHWATER

ROCK FORMATION RECORD-BREAKERS

RECORD	LARGEST ACTIVE VOLCANO	DEEPEST CAVE	BIGGEST FREE-STANDING ROCK
NAME	MAUNA LOA	VERYOVKINA CAVE	ULURU (AYERS ROCK)
STATISTICS	AREA 2,035 SQ MILES (5,271 KM²)	DEPTH 7,257 FEET (2,212 M)	HEIGHT 1,142 FEET (348 M)
DETAILS	COVERS HALF THE ISLAND OF HAWAII	NAMED AFTER ALEXANDER VEREVKIN, A CAVE EXPLORER	RED SANDSTONE FORMED ABOUT 600 MILLION YEARS AGO
LOCATION	HAWAII, USA	ABKHAZIA, GEORGIA	NORTHERN TERRITORY, AUSTRALIA
RECORD	OLDEST ROCK	OLDEST MOUNTAIN RANGE	LARGEST METEORITE
NAME	ACASTA GNEISS	MAKHONJWA MOUNTAINS	THE HOBA METEORITE
STATISTICS	AGE ABOUT 4 BILLION YEARS OLD	HEIGHT UP TO 5,900 FEET (1,800 M) ABOVE SEA LEVEL	WEIGHS OVER 58 TONS (60 METRIC TONS)
DETAILS	DISCOVERED ON SHORES OF THE REMOTE ACASTA RIVER	AGE 3.6 BILLION YEARS OLD	DISCOVERED IN 1920
LOCATION	NORTHWEST TERRITORIES, CANADA	SOUTH AFRICA	NAMIBIA

GEMS & PRECIOUS METALS RECORD-BREAKERS

RECORD	LARGEST GOLD NUGGET	LARGEST UNCUT DIAMOND	MOST VALUABLE GEMSTONE
NAME	THE WELCOME STRANGER	THE CULLINAN DIAMOND	THE HOPE DIAMOND
STATISTICS	WEIGHED 156 LB (70.9 KG)	WEIGHED 3,106 CARATS (621 GRAMS OR 22 OUNCES)	ESTIMATED VALUE OF US $250 MILLION (£200 MILLION)
DATE OF DISCOVERY	DISCOVERED IN 1869	MINED IN 1905	DISCOVERED IN 1812
LOCATION	AUSTRALIA	SOUTH AFRICA	FOUND IN INDIA; CURRENTLY IN USA
RECORD	RAREST GEM MINERAL	RAREST METAL	LARGEST PLATINUM NUGGET
NAME	PAINITE	FRANCIUM	NO NAME
STATISTICS	A FEW THOUSAND SPECIMENS HAVE BEEN FOUND	IT IS RADIOACTIVE AND ONLY A FEW TENS OF GRAMS EXIST ON EARTH AT ANY TIME	WEIGHT: 22 LB (9.7 KG)
DATE OF DISCOVERY	DISCOVERED IN 1950S	DISCOVERED IN 1939	DISCOVERED 1843
LOCATION	MYANMAR	EARTH'S CRUST	URAL MOUNTAINS, RUSSIA